Wanderings in China

Constance Frederica "CF" Gordon-Cumming was born in Scotland in 1837, the twelfth child of a wealthy aristocratic family. The Gordon-Cummings were seemingly all travellers and explorers – planters in Sri Lanka, explorers of the River Nile, travellers to the Canadian interior, and at least one big-game hunter in Africa. Gordon-Cumming's first venture in foreign travel was a visit to her sister, who had married an officer stationed in India. She was a keen observer and self-taught landscape painter. *Wanderings in China* was first issued as two volumes in 1886.

Paul French, who has introduced and annotated this reprint, was born in London and lived and worked in Shanghai for many years. His book *Midnight in Peking* was a *New York Times* bestseller and a BBC Radio 4 Book of the Week.

Also by Paul French:

Destination Peking

Strangers on the Praia

Destination Shanghai

City of Devils: A Shanghai Noir

Midnight in Peking: How the Murder of a Young Englishwoman Haunted the Last Days of Old Peking

The Badlands: Decadent Playground of Old Peking

Bloody Saturday: Shanghai's Darkest Day

Supreme Leader: The Making of Kim Jong-un

Betrayal in Paris: How the Treaty of Versailles Led to China's Long Revolution

The Old Shanghai A-Z

Through the Looking Glass: China's Foreign Journalists from Opium Wars to Mao

Carl Crow – A Tough Old China Hand: The Life, Times, and Adventures of an American in Shanghai

North Korea Paranoid Peninsula – A Modern History

Wanderings in China

Hong Kong and Canton, Christmas and New Year, 1878/1879

By Constance Frederica "CF" Gordon-Cumming (1886)

Annotated by Paul French

BLACKSMITH BOOKS

China Revisited: No. 2 of a series

Wanderings in China

ISBN 978-988-75547-6-9

Published by Blacksmith Books
Unit 26, 19/F, Block B, Wah Lok Industrial Centre,
37-41 Shan Mei Street, Fo Tan, Hong Kong
Tel: (+852) 2877 7899
www.blacksmithbooks.com

Cover photo: Roadside food, fruit and vegetable pedlars and
street kitchen, Hong Kong. Photograph attributed to Lai Fong
(Afong Studio). Image courtesy of Special Collections,
University of Bristol Library, DM2520/1 (www.hpcbristol.net).
Many thanks to Jamie Carstairs and Robert Bickers of the
Historical Photographs of China project at the University
of Bristol.

CONTENTS

ABOUT CHINA REVISITED

China Revisited is a series of extracted reprints of mid-nineteenth to early-twentieth century Western impressions of Hong Kong, Macao and China. The series comprises excerpts from travelogues or memoirs written by missionaries, diplomats, military personnel, journalists, tourists and temporary sojourners. They came to China from Europe or the United States, some to work or to serve the interests of their country, others out of curiosity. Each excerpt is fully annotated to best provide relevant explications of Hong Kong, Macao and China at the time, to illuminate encounters with historically interesting characters or notable events.

Given the prejudices of the era, what are we to take from these works? Some have a stated agenda, namely colonial control and administration of Hong Kong and Macao, or else proselytising and saving souls for the Christian religion. This is generally obvious in the writing. Others have no stated objective but impressions of the regions, their peoples, and cultures are products of their time and value systems. There is an unsurprising tendency to exoticize, make generally unfavourable comparisons to their home cultures and societies, and to misunderstand what they are witnessing.

They are – whether from American or European sources – invariably from men and women of some formal education. Their acquaintances are among the colonial authorities and foreign diplomats. These "filters" mean that invariably we are given an elite view of China; this is not the experience of the non-officer class sailor, merchant seaman, regular soldier, or working-class visitor. Even before we get to racial prejudice we are encountering class prejudice.

The writers in this series were all men and women of their time, encountering China at specific times in its history. Most of them were visitors or residents for a limited amount of time. However, some, notably the missionaries, did remain for longer – decades in some cases. In general the only foreigners who had credible local language skills were the missionaries, or British colonial district officers and their Portuguese equivalents in Macao, along with some diplomat-scholars. Assumptions were made, prejudices voiced, yet all of these writings have something to reveal of the encounters from which they derived.

FOREWORD

"I have fled southwards with swallows"

The excerpts from Constance Gordon-Cumming's *Wanderings in China* included here all come from the first volume of the William Blackwood & Sons 1886 edition, the first. Similarly so the illustrations included. The two volumes generally take the form of a series of diary entries. I have included those parts I think of most interest to contemporary readers and have largely excluded sections that are either arcane or dwell on divisions within the Christian religion and offer no impression of Hong Kong or Guangzhou. Where I have skipped paragraphs, I have inserted three ellipses (***) to indicate this process.

The excerpts included here cover Christmas 1878 and the terrible "Great Fire" of Hong Kong that swept through the Central and Mid-Levels districts; her explorations of the city of Canton and its environs in early January 1879; her experiences of the Chinese New Year festivities in Canton in late January 1879; and finally her return to Hong Kong for the horse races at Happy Valley in February 1879.

I have at some points taken the decision to omit several sentences that contain outdated racial stereotypes or comments that offer nothing to our understanding of either Hong Kong or Guangzhou in the 1870s. Unusually for the late Victorian period Constance Gordon-Cumming is a heavy user of the exclamation mark. I have left them in to show, perhaps interestingly, just what the author thought worthy of exclamation.

INTRODUCTION

Eka's Wanderings

Constance Frederica "Eka" Gordon-Cumming was born in Scotland in 1837, the twelfth child of a wealthy and well-travelled family. She was privately tutored at home and had a Swiss governess who taught her French. The extended Gordon-Cumming family were seemingly all travellers and explorers – planters in Sri Lanka, explorers of the River Nile, travellers to the Canadian interior, and at least one big-game hunter in Africa. Her first tours as a girl were through the Scottish Highlands and Islands. On these trips to the north of Scotland she became an accomplished, and largely self-taught, landscape painter.

Wanderings in China was first issued as two volumes in 1886 by William Blackwood & Sons, a well-known publisher based in Edinburgh and London. The book was regularly updated with a major new edition in 1900.

Gordon-Cumming's trips to China yielded several works. Having published *Wanderings in China* she then wrote *Notes on China and its Missions,* published in 1889 by the Church Missionary Society (CMS, a British society founded in 1799 with missions around the world including in Guangzhou, Hong Kong and Shanghai).

She had first visited Peking in 1879 and met William Hill Murray, a Scottish missionary to China who had invented the Numeral Type system, through which blind and illiterate Chinese learned to read and write. Gordon-Cumming became a great supporter of Hill Murray's and wrote a pamphlet extolling his invention and achievements, *Work for the Blind in China* (1892). She carried on trying to raise awareness of the issue of the blind in China and wrote a tract on the situation of the blind there.[1]

***

After her death in 1924 the London *Times* published a lengthy obituary of Constance Gordon-Cumming:

Obituary
Miss Gordon-Cumming

Miss CF Gordon-Cumming, whose death is announced elsewhere, was one of the most travelled ladies of the last century. Although she

---

1   *The Blind in China*, privately published in Helensburgh in 1895.

was in no sense an explorer, still the narratives of her widespread travels, written with humour and intelligent observation, did much to diffuse among the general reading public a knowledge of countries of which most people were fairly ignorant. In 1904 she published her "Autobiography", which is full of interest. She had very fair artistic taste and produced, as the result of her wide wanderings, many sketches, both in black-and-white and in colour, which she was always ready to exhibit whenever desired to do so. She was a woman of great vigour, both of body and of mind, and was always a welcome companion to her many friends and acquaintances.

Constance Frederica Gordon-Cumming was born at Altyre, in Morayshire, on May 24, 1837, the twelfth of the 15 children of Sir William Gordon-Cumming, second baronet, and head of the Clan Cumming, or Comyn. The Comyns played a great part in the early days of Scottish history, and Miss Gordon-Cumming was proud of her ancestry, which she traced back to Charlemagne. By inter-marriage they were related to many of the leading Scottish families and not a few of those of England. Miss Gordon-

Cumming tells us she "started in life with 50 first cousins, about twice as many second and third cousins, and collaterals without number, for the family tree had roots and branches ramifying in every direction; and as each group centred round some more or less notable house it followed that England and Scotland were dotted over with points of family interest in those good old days when it was held that 'blood is thicker than water,' and kinship, however much diluted. was freely recognized."

She spent her early years at Altyre amid beautiful and happy surroundings. Her brother, Roualeyn Gordon-Cumming, the celebrated South African lion-hunter, was 17 years older than his sister, and his return when she was six years old was a great event. Other brothers made their way to India, Ceylon, and other parts of the world, so that she may be said to have been brought up in an atmosphere of travel and adventure. At the age of six "Eka" as she was called, went to live at Cresswell Hall, Northumberland, with her eldest sister, who had married Oswald Baker Cresswell. From here she was sent to school in London, where at intervals she spent several years. After the death of her father in 1854,

Miss Gordon-Cumming lived with relatives in Northumberland, London, the Highlands, and elsewhere. Thus she passed her life until in 1868 at the age of 31, she made, with much hesitation, her first venture in foreign travel by paying a visit to her sister, who had married an officer stationed in India. She took ample advantage of her opportunities to visit much that was worth seeing in India, including the Himalayas. here she had what she called a "a year of enchantment." On her return she recorded her experiences and impressions in her first publication, "From the Hebrides to the Himalayas," a bulky work, afterwards divided into two – "In the Hebrides" and "In the Himalayas and on Indian Plains". On her visit to India, she was able to get a glimpse of the attractions of Ceylon. Her desire to see more of the island was gratified in 1872 when on the invitation of her old friends she visited the island and the results were published in her "Two Happy Years in Ceylon."

Miss Gordon-Cumming made no pretensions to be an explorer, like Mrs Bishop (Miss Isabella Bird) and other adventurous ladies of the 19th and 20th centuries.[2] But the first two records of her travels show her to have been a keen observer, interested in many of the aspects of the regions she traversed—in the geography, their geology, their people, and their works, their beliefs, superstitions, and folk-lore, in social and political conditions—so that her narratives, full of brightness and humour and human sympathy, were for the time substantial contributions to knowledge. She had been home only for a few months when she had the opportunity of visiting Fiji, which had been handed over by the chiefs to the Great White Queen. In March, 1875, she accompanied the first Governor, Sir Arthur Hamilton Gordon (the first Lord Stanmore), and his party.[3] *En route* she spent some weeks at Sydney, arriving at Fiji in September. Here she spent the next two years, of which "every day was full of interest and novelty," as recorded in her narrative "At Home in Fiji," including her experiences of a visit to New Zealand. It was

---

2   Isabella Lucy Bishop, née Bird (1831-1904), nineteenth-century British explorer, writer, photographer and naturalist who visited China in 1878 and 1897.

3   Arthur Charles Hamilton-Gordon, 1st Baron Stanmore (1829-1912), British Liberal Party politician and colonial administrator.

in 1877, while in Fiji, that she was offered the opportunity of a voyage in the Pacific in a French man-of-war, visiting Tahiti, Tonga, Samoa, and other groups, finishing up in California. The result was one of her most interesting narratives, "A Lady's Cruise in a French Man-of-War". Her six months in California furnished her with material for her "Granite Crags of California". In August, 1878, she left San Francisco for Japan, where she spent several months, the only account of which is contained in her "Memories" (1904), occupying five chapters full of interest on many aspects of Japanese life. From Japan she passed on to China, to which she devoted six months, the story of which is told in her "Wanderings in China". In September 1879, she returned to San Francisco with General Ulysses Grant and his family.[4] From San Francisco she visited the Hawaiian Islands, where, among her other experiences, she climbed the great volcano Mauna Loa, many aspects of which she recorded in those sketches which formed some of the most

---

4   Ulysses S. Grant (1822-1885), an American soldier and politician who served as the eighteenth president of the United States.

attractive and instructive results of her worldwide travels.

Altogether what Miss Gordon-Cumming accomplished in those years of almost incessant travel is remarkable, and her voluminous records of the results, not only in books but in dozens of magazine articles, are far above the flimsy narratives of the mere globetrotter. On her return she took up her residence at Crieff, and there she remained for the rest of her life, devoting herself to her neighbours, rich and poor, and her numerous relations. She also spent much time in developing the invention of the numeral type for the use of illiterate Chinese, both blind and seeing.[5]

5 'Obituary – Miss Gordon-Cumming', *The Times* (London), September 5, 1924.

Ever yours truly
Constance F. ᵉᵏᵃ Gordon Cumming

WANDERINGS IN CHINA

(VOLUME 1)

(This text and spellings taken from *Wanderings in China* by CF Gordon-Cumming, Edinburgh and London: William Blackwood and Sons, 1886)

A MEMORABLE CHRISTMAS

HONG-KONG

Care of Mrs Snowden, City of Victoria
Isle of Hong-Kong,
Christmas-Day, 1878.

Certainly fortune has favoured me, for we reached this most lovely city early this morning, and have had a most enjoyable Christmas-day. I had not the remotest conception that I was coming to anything so beautiful;

so, when with the earliest light of dawn, we slowly – very slowly – steamed into this exquisite harbour, its beauty, so suddenly revealed, left me mute with delight. Perhaps the contrast between these encircling ranges of shapely hills and the dead level of the Shanghai coast, help to make these seem more impressive. Certainly I have seen no harbour to compare with this, though I suppose Rio Janeiro claims the palm of beauty above all others.[6]

This is like a great inland lake, so entirely do the jagged mountain-ranges of the mainland and the island of Kowlung seem to close around the Rocky Isle, whose great city bears the name of England's Queen, and from whose crowning peak floats the Union Jack.[7] The said peak is really only 1825 feet in height.[8] Though it looks so imposing, it is simply the termination of the ridge which forms the backbone of the isle and along whose base extends the city – a granite city, hewn from the granite mountains, with granite fortifications, granite drains to provide for the rush of the summer rains; everything seems to be granite, but yet there is nothing cold in its appearance, for all is gilded by the mellow sunlight. All

---

6   (sic) Rio de Janeiro.

7   Cumming means Kowloon peninsula and the 'great city that bears the name of England's Queen' being the City of Victoria, roughly akin to today's Central District.

8   Or thereabouts…

the principal houses have lovely shrubberies, with fine ornamental trees, which soften the effect, and make each terraced road seem delightful.

There is so very little, if any, level ground, save what has been reclaimed artificially, that steep streets of stairs lead from the business quarters on the sea embankment right up the face of the hill, the lower spurs of which are all dotted over with most luxurious houses and shady gardens, now gay with camellias and roses and scarlet poinsettias. And in the midst of it all is the loveliest Botanical Garden, beautifully laid out, and where all the rich and rare forms of foliage, from tropical or temperate climes, combine to produce a garden of delight, whence you look down upon the emerald green and dazzling blue of this beautiful harbour, where a thousand vessels, and boats and junks without number, can ride in absolute safety.[9]

I had a glimpse of it all this afternoon, but indeed it would be difficult to obtain a more entrancing view than from this house itself, which really belongs to Sir John Small, the Chief-Justice, but, in his absence, is tenanted by Mr Snowden, the acting Chief-Justice, who, on the strength of a letter from Sir Harry Parkes (one of the many acts of kindness for which I am indebted to him),

---

9 Fully the Hong Kong Zoological and Botanical Gardens founded in 1864 and opened to the public in 1871.

came to offer me a welcome to Hong-Kong, and to this lovely home.[10]

But I must tell you first of our arrival. My fellow-passenger from Japan, Miss Shervinton, had come to rejoin her father and we waited a little while expecting to see him appear.[11] But being impatient to get ashore, we chartered a sampan, i.e., a covered boat, inhabited by a whole Chinese family consisting of a long-tailed father, four funny little children, and a comely mother with beautifully dressed glossy hair, a comfortable blouse, and very loose short trousers, showing neat firm feet and

---

10   Either through a typo or misremembering, Gordon-Cumming refers to "Sir John Small" when she means Sir John Jackson Smale (1805-1882). Smale was a British lawyer and judge, appointed Attorney General of Hong Kong in 1860, a member of the Legislative Council in 1861 and Lord Chief-Justice 1866-1881 (though he also retained his lucrative private practice). The Honourable Francis Snowden, Acting Chief Justice from 1874, was promoted to Acting Colonial Secretary in 1879. Sir Harry Parkes (1828-1885) had been in China since 1841 and had a sensational career as a translator and diplomat, spending periods of time at Nanjing, Shanghai and Guangzhou. He had also spent time in the Kingdom of Siam (Thailand) and in northern China during the Second Opium War. His later career took him to Japan and Korea. He died in Beijing.

11   One of four daughters of Lieutenant Colonel Shervinton of the 46th Regiment, a veteran of the Crimean War (1853-1856), stationed at Hong Kong periodically.

ankles. Not having previously been in a sampan, I was glad to begin the day with a new experience!

We met Colonel Shervinton almost as soon as we landed and we all went together to breakfast at the principal hotel, and thence to the Cathedral, which, though not to be compared in beauty with that at Shanghai, is a fine roomy church.[12] There is a surplice choir, but the Christmas decorations are of a severe type, being confined to flowers in pots on the chancel-steps and round the font. A full congregation, and a nice hearty service, with sermon by Bishop Burdon (the Bishop of this diocese of Victoria) who, though still in the prime of life, is the fortunate possessor of such snow-white locks and beard as must surely be accounted a special episcopal endowment in a land where even grey hair commands such special honour as in China![13]

---

12   The Cathedral Church of Saint John the Evangelist, St. John's. I assume Gordon-Cumming is comparing St. John's to Gilbert Scott's Holy Trinity Church in Shanghai. St. John's is Decorated Gothic in style and Holy Trinity is slightly later Gothic Revival.

13   John Shaw Burdon (1826-1907), Scottish missionary with the Church Missionary Society (CMS). He spent some years evangelising in Shanghai and on nearby Chongming Island where he became fluent in Shanghai dialect. He was appointed Bishop of the South China Diocese of the Anglican Church in 1874 based in Hong Kong. He was somewhat controversial with some in the British community in Hong Kong and China,

We returned to the hotel for luncheon, immediately after which, in prompt answer to letters from various friends in Japan, came several most kind residents, inviting me to their homes. Fortunately for me, the first to arrive was Mr Snowden (fortunately, I mean, because this house is so beautifully situated some way up the hill, overlooking the whole town and harbour, whereas the other quarters, so cordially offered to me, lay in the town itself).

Having despatched my luggage, Mr Snowden took me for a turn through the crowded business parts of the city – the Chinese and the Portuguese quarters – all built in terraces along horizontal streets, but connected one with another by steep streets of stairs. There is a specially picturesque spot right below the house, where five Chinese and Portuguese streets meet.

From this crowded centre we went on to a very different scene, namely, the beautiful gardens, where we revelled in the fragrance of flowers bathed in sunlight, and as we wandered through shady bamboo-groves, or stood beneath the broad shadow of great banyan-trees, at every turn we caught glimpses of white sails floating on the calm blue harbour far below us, reflecting the cloudless blue of heaven – a scene of most perfect peace,

---

having opposed Britain's involvement in both the First and Second Opium Wars.

with never a jarring sound to suggest the busy bustling life, and all the noise of the city.

In short, I have already seen enough to convince me that it would be difficult to find more fascinating winter quarters than this oft-abused city. As to climate, although in the same latitude as Calcutta, it is far cooler, and whatever it may be in June or July, to-day it is delicious and balmy, like the sweetest summer day in England; and I am told that this is a fair sample of the whole winter at Hong-Kong, and that for five consecutive months there will probably not be even a shower! Only think what a paradise for an artist! Every day at the same hour the identical lights and shadows, and any number of willing and intelligent coolies ready to fetch and carry him and his goods, and save him all physical fatigue!

We arrived here in time to find Mrs Snowden waiting to welcome me to cosy five o'clock tea in the pretty English drawing-room. In short, everything is so pleasant that already I have begun to feel myself quite at home in this British isle of Hong-Kong. Now it is time to dress for dinner. Every one here seems to have a dinner-party to-night.

I seem to have lived many days since writing so far. I can hardly realise that it was only the night before last that my impressions of Hong-Kong were all so peaceful and so calm, for ever since we have been surrounded with so wild a turmoil, and a scene of such awful dread, that it feels as if we had been living in a dream.

Surely never before has Christmas so vividly exemplified the familiar words of its church service, which tell of the battle with "burning and fuel of fire!"[14]

On Christmas night, just as the guests were preparing to leave at 11P.M., suddenly a startling sound of sharp clanging rang through the night. The others knew well what it meant, and I was not long left in doubt. It was the fire-alarm! We all ran to the verandah, which, as I have told you, overlooks the whole town and harbour. These lie outspread below, as it were, the base of a great amphitheatre.

We had, a few moments before, been noticing what a calm beautiful scene it was, with its thousand points of gleaming light, the reflections of the glittering stars overhead, blending with those of the vessels floating on the still waters, and all the lights of the city – stationary

---

14   First lesson for Christmas Day – Isaiah ix. 5. [This is Gordon-Cumming's own footnote].

and locomotive, the latter indicating the paper lanterns carried by all wayfarers and chair-coolies.

Now a new feature was added to the scene. From the very point where the five streets met, rose a tall column of fiery smoke, with shooting tongues of flame. Another moment and the gentlemen had rushed off, some being members of the fire-brigade, and others having a very personal interest in the danger which might so quickly approach their own offices.

The alarm-bells rang on more and more wildly – sharp jangling bells, which once heard could never be forgotten, so unlike any other peal is that affrighted clanging – no seasonable Christmas chimes, but an awful appeal; a far-reaching sound that should summons all the engines from every corner of the city, and all men enlisted in the brigades, from their festivities. These, as a rule, pride themselves on the extraordinary rapidity with which they respond to such a call, and many a fire has been quenched at the very outset, owing to the velocity with which its first indication has been smothered.

But, of course, on this night everything was a little lax. Many men had been dining with friends at some distance from the city, and it was near midnight ere they could get back. Others returned unsuspectingly to find the awful havoc that had taken place. So the bells tolled on in wild appeal, and those of the Roman Catholic

Cathedral took up the alarm, while fire-drums beat in the streets to hasten the laggards, and meanwhile the smoke-clouds grew denser and more dense, and, to make matters worse, a sharp breeze sprang up from the north, fanning the flames, and carrying sparks and burning fragments to ignite new buildings at a distance.[15]

There is little doubt that the fire was the work of an incendiary. It began in the store of a small general dealer – an Englishman. He was absent, and when the place was broken open, the whole was found saturated with kerosine *(sic)*. It is also believed that some men spread the fire to their own stores for the sake of the insurance money. Curiously enough three fires broke out simultaneously on other parts of the isle; but there really seems to have been no object to make it appear that these were incendiary, as there was no general attempt at looting. On the contrary, every one appeared half stupefied, as the flames rapidly gained the mastery, suddenly bursting from fresh houses here and there, where least suspected, and spreading from street to street.

---

15   The second Cathedral of the Immaculate Conception at the junction of Pottinger Street and Wellington Street built to replace a previous Cathedral destroyed by fire in 1859. In the 1880s a third cathedral was built on Caine Road, Mid-Levels, to allow for a larger congregation.

That livelong night we stood or sat on the verandah watching this appallingly magnificent scene – the flames rising and falling, leaping and dancing, now bursting from some fresh house, shooting up in tongues of fire, now rolling in dense volumes of black smoke. Now it was a paraffine *(sic)*-store which blazed with fierce light, and, a moment later, a New Year store of fireworks were all aflame, shooting and exploding all on their own account.

From house to house, and from street to street the beautiful, terrible Fire-Demon swept on its destroying path, for the flames, now fanned by a keen breeze, rushed hungrily on, sometimes sweeping right across a street to devour the opposite houses, – sometimes, for some reason utterly incomprehensible, working right round a block, and leaving one or two houses in the very heart of the conflagration utterly untouched (like the Three Children in the fiery furnace).[16]

---

16   Presumably a reference to the story of Shadrach, Meshach and Abednego, figures from chapter 3 of the Book of Daniel in the Bible. Three Hebrew men (though often portrayed as younger children in artistic renditions) are thrown into a fiery furnace by Nebuchadnezzar, King of Babylon, after they refuse to bow down to the king's image. The three are preserved from harm and the king sees four men walking in the flames, "the fourth ... like a son of God".

From our high post we looked down on the awful sea of fire, watching it work onward, – stealing under roofs – lighting in a rain of fire on distant houses where we could see sparks smouldering on some weak corner of a roof or an inflammable verandah – then would come a little puff of smoke, followed by a burst of flame, and then would come another outburst in quite a different part of the town, till so many places were blazing at once, that the firemen were utterly baffled.

Very soon it was evident that neither their numerical strength, their engines, nor their meagre water-supply could possibly master the fire – a very startling revelation to the colony, which prided itself on the perfect organisation of its fire-brigade. Whether the actual water-supply was insufficient, or whether the engines were not sufficiently powerful, seems uncertain; but even when they were got to work, the puny jets failed to reach the top of the loftier houses, and where once the fire had fairly obtained a footing, any attempt at extinguishing it was so obviously hopeless, that the firemen's efforts were chiefly directed to saving the neighbouring or opposite buildings, by tearing down the verandahs and all the woodwork, and by covering the walls with carpets, curtains, or matting, and endeavouring to keep these saturated.

Among the houses thus saved is the Oriental Bank, in which I take a special interest, because had Mr Snowden reached me five minutes later this afternoon, I should at this moment be the guest of Mrs Crombie at the said bank, and instead of being safely housed here (we *believe* this house is now safe!).[17] I should have been sharing her night of awful anxiety.[18] The room which I should have occupied is now saturated with the water-jets thrown on, as a preventative means while houses close by were blazing. The whole opposite side of the street was burnt, and only by super-human efforts was the bank saved, the whole outside being hung as aforesaid, with mats and carpets, which were incessantly pumped upon. Of course preparations for the worst were made, and the wife, and other treasure, were sent to safe quarters on land and sea. I believe that all the banks sent their treasure and valuable papers on board one of the men-of-war lying in harbour.

---

17   Established in Bombay as the Bank of Western India in 1842, it moved its headquarters to London, changed its name to the Oriental Bank Corporation and opened in Hong Kong in 1845. In 1847, it was the first bank in the colony to issue banknotes. Under pressure from new entrants in the 1880s, notably the Hongkong and Shanghai Banking Corporation, the Oriental Bank ceased operations in 1892.

18   DAJ Crombie, Agent of the Oriental Bank Corporation, Queen's Road, Hong Kong. In 1879 Crombie moved to be the agent of the bank in Yokohama, Japan. Crombie did well for himself, having started in Hong Kong as a humble cashier.

A large force of blue-jackets and of military came to the assistance of the firemen, and did right hearty work, though perhaps with less success than would have been the case on any other night.[19] Unfortunately men were on leave for their Christmas night, and not only was it difficult to collect these for organised work under any recognised leader, but a considerable number were none the steadier for their Christmas festivities, and so a good deal of British valour was misapplied.

The chief point in which the lack of generalship revealed itself, was when it became evident that the only possible means of staying the progress of the fire lay in blowing up whole blocks of houses, in order to save worse loss. But no one present would take the responsibility of giving the necessary commands.

The Commander of the Forces placed all his men (74th Highlanders and artillerymen) at the disposal of the authorities for this service, and there they stood at ease, waiting for the orders that no one could give; and meanwhile the fire did NOT wait, but swept onward quite unceremoniously, and devoured everything to right and to left. Nothing was safe in any direction, for the breeze varied in the most unaccountable manner, suddenly shifting from north-east round by north to north-west, so while some houses were saved almost miraculously,

19   Blue Jackets being Royal Marines.

others that had deemed themselves out of harm's way were suddenly aflame.

At last, after orders and counter-orders had been so freely given that the willing workers were fairly bewildered, the tardy decision was made, and then a good many houses were blown up every here and there, almost always too late to save those beyond. Besides which, the luckless owners of course tried to save as much of their furniture as possible, so that piles of inflammable stuff (invariably capped with a lot of wicker chairs!) were heaped up in the streets, forming an excellent lead for the fire, as of course a chance spark almost invariably ignited these heaps.

And so the awful flames gained intensity, and we watched them pass away from the poor densely crowded Chinese town to the larger houses of Portuguese, Parsees, and English. In each by turn we watched first the destruction of pleasant verandahs, then the gutting of the interior, revealed by the flame rushing from every window, and finally with resounding crash the roof would fall in, and from the roaring furnace within, sheets of white or red flame, and lurid smoke of many colours, swept heavenward in awful grandeur.

Although the smoke and the intense colour made it difficult to judge accurately of relative distances, my companions were able in many cases to recognise different houses, and we could plainly discern individuals on the roofs watching for the fall of sparks which they might extinguish ere they did any damage. Oh how tantalising it was sometimes from where we stood, to see sparks fall beyond their ken, and lie quickly developing, when literally within their reach, could they but have perceived them.

Amongst all the confused noises – the roar of human voices, the yelling and shouting of the Chinese rabble – the crackling and rush of flames, the crash of falling timbers, and the occasional blasting of houses with gunpowder or dynamite, there was one oft-recurring sound which, for a while, puzzled me exceedingly, till I learnt that it was a familiar sound at every Chinese festival, namely, the firing of crackers. Thousands and tens of thousands of these must have gone off. Many doubtless were offered by the frightened people to propitiate the Fire Dragon, but vast numbers were stored ready for the New Year festival.[20]

There was one moment of gorgeous scenic effect when the flames caught a great timber-merchant's yard, wherein was stored a vast accumulation of seasoned wood and firewood, which of course became a sheet of fire glowing at white heat. You can imagine with what breathless excitement we watched the deadly hard-fought

---

20   Chinese New Year 1879 (a Rabbit year) was early, coming on January 22nd.

battle betwixt fire and water, in which fire seemed to be getting so entirely the best of it.

For a long time it spread with almost equal strength in two opposite directions; but the wind urged it most fiercely in the direct line of the magnificent houses of the great merchant princes, many of whom (at least the women folk) spent the night in packing such of their most precious valuables as there seemed some chance of saving. It did not take me long to repack mine, and my hostess only collected her chief treasures, as it really seemed hopeless to commence work, with such an accumulation of beautiful curios, and the conviction that if this house did take fire, it would be impossible to get coolies to carry our goods, and indeed, we knew not where to seek safety.

But certainly we were in considerable danger, for the fiery smoke swept right over our heads, and fell in a hail of sparks and blazing fragments all about the place; and at any moment one of these alighting on the woodwork, and there smouldering unnoticed, or else falling on the flimsy Chinese houses just beyond this garden wall, would have placed this house in frightful jeopardy.

Owing to the infatuated delay in not blowing up houses till they were actually on fire, the Civil Hospital was entirely destroyed, though happily no lives were lost, the patients being carried to another hospital.[21] There was a time of awful anxiety as the fire swept on directly towards the jail, wherein are stowed five hundred prisoners – scoundrels of the worst type. A strong military guard were on duty to guard the prison, and remove the prisoners in case of need.[22] Had this become necessary, they had orders to shoot any who attempted to escape, as they would inevitably become leaders of a terrible lot of scoundrels of all sorts who are said to have drifted here, escaping from Canton and other cities where supervision is more rigid, in order to profit by the exceeding leniency of the present Government of Hong-Kong. I am told that they keep the police exceedingly busy, though they number about six hundred, and a very fine body they are. There are three distinct lots of these guardians of the peace, each with a distinctive uniform. There are genuine British "bobbies," Chinamen, and Sikhs – the latter a very picturesque body, with their blue uniform, red turban, and high boots. In addition to all these public servants,

21 The Civil Hospital was opened in a converted missionary bungalow in 1850. The hospital was designed primarily to cater to government/colonial officials, police and prisoners. It was expanded in 1859 to provide fee-paying Europeans and Chinese, and vagrants of any nationality, with western-style medicine.

22 Victoria Gaol, built in 1841 and partially remaining as part of the Tai Kwun development on Hollywood Road.

every householder of any standing keeps a private patrol to guard his home and his offices.

Very near the jail lies the Roman Catholic Cathedral, and this was also in dire jeopardy; in fact, some sparks alighting on the roof did ignite one corner, which, however, was quickly extinguished by hand service with buckets.[23] No jet from the feeble engines could have reached so high.

Of course the tremendous glare lighted up the great buildings and the mountains all round with a hot red glow, while intervening towers and spires stood out in black relief against the red light, or the cold steely grey of harbour and sky. I never could have conceived a scene so awful and yet so wonderfully beautiful. All night it was like a succession of pictures in the style of Martin's "Destruction of Jerusalem," or "The Last Day." Then morning broke – first a cold grey, just clearing the mountains as round the harbour; and then the rosy dawn, gradually changing to the mellow sunlight, which, while it revealed the full measure of the night's ravages, yet gilded the smoke-clouds, transforming the beautiful fire-illumined darkness into the lovely panorama of yesterday; only in the centre lay a confused mass of dark ruin veiled by filmy blue or white smoke and tremulous mirage of hot air playing above the smouldering ruins, while here and

---

23   See footnote 15 above.

there a denser volume of black wicked smoke indicated where the mischief was still spreading.

It is a frightful confession to make, but any artist will sympathise when I say, that as each picture thus presented seemed more gorgeously effective than the last, I positively again and again found myself forgetting its horror in the ecstasy of its beauty! It really felt as if we were sitting luxuriously in the dress circle watching some wondrous panoramic play, with amazingly realistic scenic effects!

For seventeen hours the fire raged on with unabated might, till it had made a clean sweep of about four hundred houses, covering about ten acres of ground, and leaving thousands of poor creatures homeless.

Even hours after we thought all was safely over, flames suddenly burst from one more large house just beyond the hospital; it was entirely consumed, and the heaps of ruin still smoulder, sending up dense volumes of white smoke, and ready to break out at a thousand spots.

As soon as the fire ceased (which it did apparently of its own free will, as both the cathedral and the jail offered an easy prey), Mr Snowden took me down to the town, and we went over a great part of the ruined city, and a truly heartrending sight it was. In every corner of the unburnt streets whole families were huddled together beside a little pile of the poor household stuff they had succeeded in saving, while the houses, which a few hours earlier had been homes, lay in smouldering ruins. I never could have believed that any community could have borne so awful a calamity so bravely and patiently. Not a murmur was heard; not a tear have I seen shed by women who have lost everything, and crouched, shivering and half-dressed, in a really chilling breeze.

But they seem to have a curiously suspicious and by no means flattering feeling towards such kindly Britons as wish to help them, various offers of assistance and loan of blankets having been flatly declined by women whose children were crying with cold.

One very remarkable instance of this is, that the captain of the *Perusia*, a large vessel now lying in harbour, offered good quarters to upwards of six hundred of the houseless Chinese sufferers. The offer was made through the Tung Wah Hospital Committee, who regulate all such matters for their countrymen, and these positively refused the good offer, which included comfortable provision for cooking, and whatever else kindness could have bestowed.[24] It appears that this vessel was at one time in the coolie trade, and the supposition is that the people

---

24   The Tung Wah Hospital, Hong Kong's first purpose-built hospital for the general public, built in 1870 at 12 Po Yan Street, Sheung Wan.

thought they would be kidnapped.[25] However, the Tung Wah people made no other provision for the luckless wretches, who have been all this time living in the open street, and at night are half perished with cold.

The extent of ground utterly ruined is quite awful. We walked up one street and down another, uphill and downhill by the streets of stairs, and along the horizontal streets, for between two and three hours, and even then had not gone all over the ground. It is such a scene of desolation that I find it hard to realise that these are the very streets which on Christmas-day I saw crowded with comfortable-looking people. Now there are only a few blackened walls, and engines are still pumping vigorously on the mountains of fallen bricks, which in some places quite block the streets, and from which puffs of smoke still rise, as if to show that the foe is not dead, but only sleeping. It needs but a little neglect and a fresh breeze, and the chances are that the fire might break out again, and there is no saying where it would end. It would have a better chance now, for all the firemen are fairly worn

---

25 The steamer *Perusia*, owned by the American Olyphant shipping line, called regularly at Hong Kong on voyages between Peru and China. The primary intended "cargo" was Chinese labourers (referred to above by Cumming as "the coolie trade") destined for Peru. However, on a number of occasions that the firm tried to bring labourers on board they were prevented in both Hong Kong and at the port of Canton in China.

out, as are also the soldiers and sailors, who have been on duty with very small intermission for about forty hours, and who are still on guard at all points to check looting, and to prevent foolhardy people from going into danger in the neighbourhood of unsound walls. There will be an immense amount of work in even pulling these down, when they have cooled.

Mr Snowden met many of his acquaintances still in their fire-brigade helmets, all looking scorched and utterly exhausted. Several have been hurt. They say that never before has there been so disastrous a conflagration in Hong-kong.

It is marvellous to see how capricious the fire has been. Here is a street with one side intact – the other wholly destroyed; here stands part of a gable with here and there a wooden shelf unscathed, on which rest securely a few delicate china vases or some growing plants. In one house which had blazed most fiercely, I saw the verandah upstairs of lattice wood-work, alone standing intact, while the whole house was gutted, and on the verandah were arranged pots with flowers and variegated leaves not even scorched, and, just above them, from a skeleton roof, hung a paper lantern untouched!

Some of the best curio shops are burned, and it is pitiful to see the beautiful great jars smashed, and lacquer all dirt-begrimed. In one place we came on the whole stock of a poor artist-photographer (who paints wonderfully correct, if not artistic, portraits in oil, from any old photograph) all strewn over the street, where lay his careful paintings all torn and soiled. Everywhere is the same pitiful destruction, and stupefied people hanging listlessly about the smouldering wreck of their poor little property. Of course their losses strike one as more pathetic than the far larger destruction of fully insured rich men's houses.

I have just returned from a second long walk all over the scene of ruin. It has a horrible sort of attraction, even while it makes me feel sick at heart. Now I too confess to feeling utterly exhausted, though I have had nothing to do but just to sit still and watch at highest tension. And I devoutly hope never again to witness such a scene.

Hong Kong – City of Victoria

Junks and Sampans on the Min River

A Hill of Graves, Foo-Chow

City of Foo-chow: Looking Toward the Arsenal and Mount Kushan

FROM HONG-KONG TO CANTON

HONG-KONG, Wed., Jan. 1ˢᵗ, 1879.

This has been the perfection of a lovely New-Year's day. The climate here at this season is quite delicious, like a soft, balmy English summer, redolent of flowers. You can walk comfortably at any hour of the day; but the mornings and evenings are pleasantest, and then the lights are most beautiful.

In the early morning there was a very nice service at the cathedral, the bishop giving a short and practical New-Year address, followed by celebration of the Holy Communion.

Hong-kong has adopted the American custom of converting this day into a social treadmill. All ladies sit at home the livelong day to receive the calls of all the gentlemen of their acquaintance, while these rush from house to house, endeavouring to fit in the whole circle of their visiting list. Here the stream of callers began soon after breakfast, and continued all day, including all the foreign consuls, and others of divers nations – Japanese, Portuguese, Indians, French, Italian, &c.

To-night we dine at Government House, where there is to be a grand ball in honour of the New Year, and where we are to be enlivened by the pipers of the 74th and some cheery Highland reels.

Chez Mrs Lind,
Shameen, The Foreign Settlement
Canton, Jan 9th.

Embarked at 7.30 this morning, Captain Benning kindly providing me with a chair on his high deck, that I might have full enjoyment of the scenery, which in the early morning light was most beautiful.[26] Presently when we were clear of the island, he took me all over the ship to see the manner in which the Chinese passengers, to the number of about 1500, are stowed away, the more respectable class on a lower deck, and the common herd in the hold, where they are packed close as herring in a

26   This would be Savannah-born Thomas Theodore Benning Jr. (1835-1887) who joined the United States Merchant Marine and rose to the ranks of captain by working on voyages to Hong Kong before working for the Hongkong, Canton & Macao Steamboat Company.

barrel. Each stair connecting their quarters with the rest of the ship is barricaded by a heavy iron grating, securely padlocked, and at each stands a sentry with drawn sword and revolver, keeping a keen look-out down the gangway. The guard is relieved every hour. All the officers are similarly armed, and in the wheel-house are stands of arms all ready for use in case of need.

All these precautions are against the ever-present danger of pirates, who might so easily take passage among their inoffensive countrymen; in fact, these measures have been adopted in consequence of a pirate band having thus seized the S.S. *Spark*, murdered the captain and some of the officers and passengers, and made good their escape with a lot of specie. Some of them were eventually recaptured, and confessed that on a previous day they had been on board this very ship with similar intent, and a boat-load of their confederates were waiting at a given point, where the attack was to be made. But just as they reached this spot, four foreign sail were in sight (a very unusual circumstance) and they were alarmed, so refrained from action. On referring to his log, Captain Benning found these four sail mentioned at this very hour, and fully realised how narrow had been their own escape.

At about eleven o'clock we passed between the Bogue Forts (dull-looking earth-works), which mark the entrance to the Pearl River.[27] (*Bogue* apparently answering to our *Aber* – "the mouth of.") The stream here is half a mile wide. About thirty miles further we passed a nine-storied pagoda, and the old town of Whampoa, and more fortifications; and steering an intricate course through an innumerable crowd of junks and sampans, we noted the richly-cultivated lands and market-gardens, which provide not only for the 1,500,000 inhabitants of Canton (some say 2,000,000), but also for the markets of Hong-Kong.[28]

The shores are dotted with villages, in each of which stands one conspicuous great solid square structure of granite, lined with brick, about four stories high. It looks like an old Border keep, but it really is the village pawn-shop, which acts as the safe store-house for everybody's property. Here in winter are deposited all summer garments, and when spring returns they are reclaimed; and as the winter garments which are then left in pawn are more valuable, the owner sometimes receives an advance of seed for sewing his crops. Here there is no prejudice against the pawning of goods. It is a regular institution of the country, and even wealthy people send their goods

---

27 Otherwise known as the Humen strait and the forts on the islands of Anunghoy and North Wangtong.

28 Whampoa is now more commonly known as Pazhou Island and home to the Pazhou (or Whampoa) Pagoda (c.1600).

here for safe keeping. Some foreigners thus dispose of their furs in the winter season. All goods are neatly packed and ticketed, and stored in pigeon-hole compartments of innumerable shelves, ranged tier above tier, to the very summit of the tall building, which is strongly protected both against fire and thieves; in fact, the latter must be mad indeed to face the danger of attacking a pawn-tower, on whose flat roof are stored not only large stones ready to be dropped on their devoted heads, but also earthenware jars full of vitriol, and syringes wherewith to squirt this terrible liquid fire! As we approached nearer and nearer to the city, the number of these great towers multiplied, and I am told that there are in Canton upwards of a hundred first-class pawn-towers, besides a multitude of second and third class, sufficiently proving how good must be their business; and it seems that notwithstanding the very high rate of interest on money lent, ranging from 20 to 36 per cent., the people prefer borrowing money from these brokers to applying to the banks.

With the exception of these numerous square towers, some fortifications, and the very imposing Roman Catholic Cathedral (abhorred by the Chinese chiefly as having been built on land unjustly appropriated by the French), we saw little, save a moderate amount of smoke, to suggest that we were approaching a mighty city – the great southern capital of the Empire – so entirely are its low level streets concealed by the forest of masts of innumerable junks and vessels of all sorts.[29] Only in the distance rose a background of low hills, which are the White Cloud range. Altogether the first impressions of Canton are in most notable contrast to those of lovely Hong-Kong.

Approaching the city, we noted the little English cemetery on a low hillock near the river, and about two o'clock we came in sight of this wondrously green isle – the Shameen, or "Sandy Face", where handsome foreign houses appear mingling with shady banyan and other trees.[30]

Among the crowd assembled on the embankment to watch the arrival of the steamer, I noticed a group of chair-coolies in pretty uniform, bearing a resplendent palanquin, which I supposed to contain some great

---

29   The Gothic-Revival Cathedral of the Sacred Heart of Jesus, also known as the "Stone House" locally, on Yide Road, Guangzhou. It was abhorred as it was built on land seized from the Chinese in 1861 by forced treaty and built with donations from French Catholics and Emperor Napoleon III. Construction began in 1861 but was not fully completed until 1888. Hence Cumming is seeing a structure that is not yet in full use.

30   Shameen being Shamian Island at the time, and since 1859, comprising two concessions – British and French – and two bridges to the mainland.

mandarin, and was considerably taken aback on learning that it had been sent for me, being the special property of my hostess – the equivalent of a carriage in England. I must honestly confess that my ideas of life in Canton were altogether *bouleversé* by this first glimpse of the luxuries of foreign life up here.[31] I had imagined that a few exiles from Hong-Kong, who could not help themselves, had, owing to the exigencies of business, to live here, picnic fashion, in the dirty city itself, which I supposed to be much on a par with the native town at Shanghai, only more picturesque. I daresay I ought to have known better, but I didn't. So it was a most startling revelation to find myself in a very smart, purely foreign settlement, as entirely isolated from the native city as though they were miles apart, instead of being only divided by a canal, which constitutes this peaceful green spot of an island.

Here is transplanted an English social life so completely fulfilling all English requirements, that the majority of inhabitants rarely enter the city! They either walk round the isle, or up and down the wide grass road, overshadowed by banyan-trees, which encircles the isle (a circuit of a mile and a half), and which is the "Rotten Row" of the island – the meeting place for all friends; but in place of horses and carriages, its interests centre in boats without

---

31   *Bouleversé* meaning upset.

number, and from this embankment those who wish to go further, embark in their own or hired boats.

A handsome English church, and large luxurious house of Italian architecture, with deep verandahs, the homes of wealthy merchants, are scattered over the isle, embowered in the shade of their own gardens; and altogether this little spot – washed on one side by the Pearl River, and on the other by the canal – is as pleasant a quarter as could be desired.[32]

It is hard to realise that, previous to the capture of Canton in 1857, a hideous mud-flat occupied the place where this green isle now lies. Having been selected as a suitable spot for foreign settlement, piles were driven into the river and filled up with sand, and on this foundation was built an embankment of solid granite, which is now the daily recreation ground of all the foreign population. But nothing that now meets the eye on this artificial island suggests the enormous labour by which this transformation was accomplished.

Indescribable, however, is the contrast between the peace and calm which here reign and the crowds and dirt and bustle of the great Chinese city, from which it is only separated by a narrow canal at two points, each bridge

---

32 The Shamian English, Protestant, Christ's Church was built in 1865 and is now known simply as the Shamian Christian Church.

being guarded by a sentry. We can saunter beneath shady trees on the canal embankment and – overlooking the closely packed house-boats which lie moored close below us – we see the busy tide of life surging on the opposite shore. I hope ere long to find myself in the midst of it, and explore all the wonders of the great city.

Saturday Night, 11th Jan.

For two whole days we have been wandering through this wonderful city, and how to describe it in sober English is more than I can tell!

Fascinating as the bazaars of Cairo to an untravelled artist! Bewildering as the thronged and narrow streets of Benares, yet differing so essentially from these as to form a totally new experience in the annals of travel, Canton stands by itself in every impression it conveys. Alike in this only, that the days spent in each of these three cities must for ever rise above the ordinary level of our memory-pictures, as some tall pagoda-tower above the plain.

What chiefly strikes one on arriving in Canton is not so much the temples (though of these there are, I believe, about eight hundred, dedicated to gods and goddesses innumerable, and all more or less richly adorned with shrines, images, fine temple-bronzes, and elaborate wood-carving). What really fascinates the eye and bewilders the mind is simply the common street-life, which, from morning till night, as you move slowly through the streets, presents a succession of pictures, each of intense interest and novelty. In all this there is life – the real life of a great busy people, and one feels that it is really an effort to turn aside from these to see any recognised "sight." In the temples there is stagnation. Their gilding and beautiful carving are defaced and incrusted with dirt; the worshippers are only occasional, for they have so very many gods, all requiring worship by turns.

But the interest of the streets cannot be surpassed, though most of them are dirty and all narrow, some being only about six feet wide! And many not exceeding eight feet! Even this is further reduced by the singular but very effective manner of hanging out sign-boards at right angles to the shops, some suspended like the signs of old English inns, and some set upright in carved and gilded stands at the corners of the shop. They are just great planks, ten to fifteen feet in height, some black, some scarlet, some blue, some white, and a few green, and on which are embossed strange characters in scarlet or gold, which, though perhaps really merely stating the name of the shop, appear to our ignorant eyes both beautiful and mysterious!

Some shops hang up a great pasteboard model of their principal goods: a satin skull-cap or a conical straw hat denote a hatter, a shoe for a shoemaker, a fan or an umbrella for the seller of these; a huge pair of spectacles or a great gilded dragon each convey their invitation to all comers. Some streets are all given over to the workers in one trade – they are all ivory-carvers, or coffin-makers, or purveyors of strange offerings for the dead or for the gods.

I believe the chief secret of the fascination of these streets lies in the fact that you see right into every shop, so that when you can turn your eyes aside from looking right along the street, and can gaze either to right or left, each shop frontage of ten feet reveals a scene which would make the fortune of the artist who could render it faithfully.

Here a shop is not merely a receptacle of articles for sale, it is also a manufactory, where, if you have leisure to linger, you can watch each process from the beginning; and if the various things in common use among these strange people strike us as quaint, much more curious is it to see them actually made.

Moreover, limited as is the space in these tiny shops each has at least three shrines set apart for family worship. At the threshold is a tablet to the Earth Gods, before which on certain evenings are set red tapers and incense-sticks. Within the home are the Ancestral Tablets, and the altar of the Kitchen God, each of which requires many offerings and an ever-burning light. A vast multitude of shops have also an altar to the God of Wealth.

As seen from the street, the central and most striking object is invariably the name of the shop, painted on a large board in gold and bright colours, with so much carving and gilding as to make it really a gorgeous object. Above this is generally placed an image or picture of some lucky sage, or the God of Wealth, while below are two gaudy fans, to which at the New-Year festival are added enormous ornaments of gold and coloured flowers, while gay lanterns of very varied form and pattern hang in front to light up the whole.

To the initiated, some of the quaint-looking characters inscribed on these gorgeous shop-boards are full of interest. Here is a wealthy merchant who gratefully acknowledges the favours of that fat God of Wealth, who occupies so conspicuous a place in his shop, and who day by day receives such devout worship. So the tall sign-post announces the house as being "Prospered by Heaven." Another declares himself to be "ten thousand times fortunate," while his neighbour claims "Never-ending Good Luck." Here we come to "Celestial Bliss," and a little further an honest soul proclaims his heart's desire in the name assumed, "Great Gains," while another announces his store as "The Market of Golden Profits."

But when we come to note the names of the streets, they really are touchingly allegorical. Here is the street of Everlasting Love, the street of Ten Thousand Beatitudes. Special streets are consecrated to "the Saluting Dragon," "the Dragon in Repose," "the Ascending Dragon." A peculiarly unfragrant street, in this unsavoury city, is characterised as the "Street of Refreshing Breezes!" The value attached to numerous descendants is suggested by the streets of "One Hundred Grandsons," and the still more auspicious "One Thousand Grandsons."

Picture to yourself a vast city, with miles and miles of such streets, all so narrow, that the blue sky overhead seems but a strip, which in many places is shut out by screens of matting or boarding, extending from roof to roof, casting deep shadows which intensify the wealth of colour below.

The streets are paved with long narrow slabs, but with no causeway for foot passengers, for riders are few and far between: and as to chairs, they block up the street, so that the patient crowd must step close to the shops to let them pass. With the exception of a few wealthy tradesmen, who indulge in silks and satins of divers colours, all the crowd are dressed in blue, and all alike have quaintly shaven heads, and a long plait of glossy black hair, which for convenience is sometimes twined round the head during work, but must always hang full length when in presence of a superior. A closely fitting black satin skull-cap is apparently an essential part of the costume of a well-dressed tradesman or domestic servant. There is no drowsiness here – all are intent on their own business, and hurry to and fro, yet never seem to jostle or even touch one another.

After the gay crowds of Japanese women and children, the predominance of men in a Chinese crowd is a very marked feature: women are comparatively few, and all are large-footed, in other words, plebian (none the worse for that in our eyes). But the ladies of the lily feet (i.e., the distorted hoofs) must remain in the seclusion of their homes, or at best, must be carried through the street in closely-covered chairs. Those we do see are very simply dressed in prune-coloured loosely-fitting clothes; but all have bare heads and black hair elaborately dressed and ornamented with clasps of imitation jadestone; most have ear-rings and bangles to match.

Young unbetrothed girls wear their hair all brushed back, and plaited in one heavy tress just like the men; but, instead of their shaven forehead, they comb the front hair right over the brow in a straight fringe. So soon as a girl is affianced she must change her style of hair-dressing, and adopt the large chignon with the eccentric twist, which is so suggestive of a teapot with its handle!

The vast majority both of men and women wear an upper garment of dark blue material, precisely the shape of an ordinary shirt (*minus* neck or wrist-hands). The peculiarity of the said shirt is that it is worn as the outer garment! This being mid-winter, the weather is supposed to be cold, so every one is wearing thickly wadded clothes, and the whole population has a general look of comfortable stoutness!

Another remarkable feature of this crowd is that almost all are on foot, except when a foreigner, a woman, or a mandarin is carried along on men's shoulders in a curious closed-up chair. The wonder is how the bearers can make their way through the crowded streets; but they keep up a constant shouting, and the patient people stand aside. So the cumbersome chair passes rapidly, unchecked by the multitude of busy tradesmen, who also hurry along, each carrying on his shoulder a pole, from which are suspended his very varied goods.

Thus a confectioner, or baker, has two large boxes, with trays of good things; a fishmonger carries two large flat tubs full of live fish, that most in favour being a long, narrow flat fish, resembling a silver sword; or perhaps he carries two trays of bleeding fish, cut up into portions suited to the humblest purses, and smeared with blood to make them look fresh and inviting. The stationary fishmongers keep their fresh-water fish alive in tubs, which are not only full of water, but through which a running stream is made to trickle ceaselessly. The locomotive butcher likewise has two trays of raw meat, divided into infinitesimal portions of dubious animals. The gardener brings his flowers and vegetables slung in two large flat baskets; the artificial florist carries his in a box with trays, and rings a sort of small bell as he goes along; and the barber carries his quaint scarlet stool, brass basin, and razors, ready to do any amount of shaving and hair-dressing in the open street.

Each of these figures is picturesque in his way; but the barber is especially so, with his broad-brimmed straw hat, and loose dark-blue trousers and blouse, which contrast so well with the bright scarlet of the very ornamental stand on which rests the brass basin. This hangs from one end of his shoulder-pole, balanced by the aforesaid scarlet stool, which is, in fact, a small pyramidal cabinet with several drawers and flat top. I should like to invest in one, as I think no one has yet thought of taking home a barber's stool as a cabinet!

Our old apple-women are represented by men selling sugar-cane, and oranges already peeled, the latter being sold for a smaller sum than the unpeeled, inasmuch as the rind is worth more for medicinal purposes than the fruit itself.

Right through the busy crowd men bearing brimming buckets of fresh water, slung from the bamboo on their shoulders, as the sole water-supply of a multitude of the citizens; and others, without any sort of warning, trot along bearing most objectionable and unfragrant uncovered buckets, inclining foreigners to believe that Chinamen were created without the sense of smell; and proving that the sanitary arrangements of the city are of the same primitive order (and with the same view to economical agriculture) as in Hong Kong, the very elaborate system of city drains being designed only to carry off superfluous water from the streets.

One singular feature in the streets of Canton is the multitude of blind beggars, who go about in strings of eight or ten together – literally the blind leading the blind. I met a gentleman the other day who assured me that he once saw six hundred of these blind beggars, all assembled to share a beneficent distribution of rice. Nor are other beggars lacking – wild, unkempt-looking creatures, who gather in picturesque groups round the clay ovens, where, on payment of infinitesimal coin, savoury food is prepared and served out to them smoking hot.

***

At present many of the provision shops to be entirely filled with ducks, split open and dried, these being evidently the correct thing to eat on New-Year's eve. The marvel is where so many ducks could have come from!

As to the fruit-shops, it may be merely the accident of the season, but it seems as if the fruiterers purposely adorned their stalls with gold and yellow fruits (this being the auspicious colour), – masses of oranges of all sorts, gourds, bananas, and especially that extraordinary lemon known as "Buddha's fingers," which does bear some resemblance to a grotesque human hand with the fingers pressed together, and is a favourite subject for soapstone and jade carvers.[33]

I wish I could give you a faint idea of a thousandth part of what I saw in yesterday's morning-walk through the principal streets of Canton, before we even began to explore its temples and other wonderful sights. This was merely an idle morning on foot, when we had leisure to look about us and watch the preparations already being made for the great New-Year festival. The tall sign-boards

---

33 Gordon-Cumming is referring here to *citrus medica var. sarcodactylis*, or the fingered citron, a fruit segmented into obvious finger-like sections, resembling those seen on some representations of Buddha. It is called Buddha's fingers, or hand, in Chinese, Japanese and Korean.

in the open streets were being adorned with festoons of crimson cloth and large tassels and bunches of gilt flowers, adding yet more colour to the scene.

A very pretty symptom of the approaching festival is the large number of peasants who come in from the country with branches of early blossoming peach, and bundles of budding sticks. These buds open in a few days, and bunches of small red, rather wax-like bells appear. Every man, however poor, and every boat on the crowded river, endeavours to have some blossom ready to greet the New Year. Pots of narcissus, chrysanthemums, and fragrant Japanese daphnes find ready customers, and the market flower-gardeners of Fa-tee obtain much custom from the rich mandarins, both for the adornment of their own houses and of their splendid guilds.[34]

We explored shops where curious masks and gorgeous crowns and other theatrical properties are manufactured. We passed by exchanges of money, whose sign is a huge string of gilt cash like those in use here, and which are worth about a thousand to a dollar[35]; and we lingered

---

34   Fa-tee (aka Fati or Fa Ti often) is now Fangcun to the southwest of Guangzhou's Central Business District. It had been a centre of market gardening, ornamental tree production and floral cultivation since the ninth century. Japanese Daphne is also known as *Daphne odora* or Winter Daphne.

35   Handily a pre-decimalisation reader of my London Library copy of *Wanderings in China* has noted in the margin

long, watching jewellers making exquisite ornaments of kingfisher's feathers, green and blue, inlaid like enamel on a gold ground. A few steps further we paused beside an ivory-carver, producing the most delicate and costly work, undisturbed by passers-by. Next we halted to see the processes of rice being husked and pounded by foot-mills, and wheat ground to flour by bullocks turning grindstones which are placed one above the other. The oxen are blindfolded to save them from giddiness.

It was so odd to be standing in the street and to look in at a narrow frontage, past a party of men quietly dining, and to see away into the long perspective of a far back store, wherein at least a dozen of these primitive bullock-mills were working in a line. Beyond the blue haze and gloom of this interior we could see bright sunlight in the inner court, where the women were spinning cotton. Then we turned into a glassblower's house, and watched the glass being blown into the form of a huge globe, and afterwards cut in pieces and flattened in a furnace.

Need I tell you how gladly we would have lingered for hours at the shops of paper-umbrella makers, fan makers, artificial-flower makers, manufacturers of quaint and beautiful lanterns, and lamps of all sorts? Coopers, carpenters, word-carvers – each had its own special

(in pencil, though still strictly against Library rules!) that an American dollar at this time was equivalent to 4/, or shillings.

interest for us. Even the tailors cutting out strange silken garments, and the washermen ironing, were novelties in the way of street scenes; and the very tallow-chandlers become picturesque in this country, with their bunches of little red candles of vegetable tallow mixed with insect wax for domestic shrines, and gorgeously ornamented ones for the use of the temples and wealthy men.

Then we come to more ivory-carvers, and more workers in kingfishers' feathers, and then a whole street for the sale of beautiful black wood furniture, which is really made of Singapore redwood, but which takes a colour and polish equal to the finest ebony, and is very much less brittle. I think the goods produced are handsomer and far more solid then the black carved furniture of Bombay. [36]

Every now and then some great man was borne past us in his heavy chair, followed by lesser men riding, while retainers on foot ran before to clear the way, a process in which they turn their long plait to a most singular purpose, namely, that of a whip, with which they strike the bystanders, as a hint to move aside quickly.

We saw a gay marriage party, the bride's chair gorgeous with scarlet and gold, and her wedding gifts carried in scarlet boxes, all supposed to be full. Soon after we met

---

36 Singapore Redwood being *Shorea curtisii,* native to southeast Asia. Bombay Blackwood items are invariably carved from Malabar teak and rosewood.

a great procession in honour of some idols, which were conveyed along in gaudy cars, and preceded by crowds of small boys carrying lanterns and banners. Then a funeral overtook us, with mourners all dressed in white, bearing the dead in the massive wooden coffin which had probably been given him many years previously by his dutiful children, and which even now was not on its way to burial, but to be laid in the City of the Dead, there to remain in its own hired house, rented at so much a month, perhaps for years, till the priests choose to announce that the auspicious moment for burial has at length arrived, when it may be laid in a horse-shoe-shaped tomb on some bleak hillside.

A VERY STRANGE CITY

Sunday Night, 12th Jan.[37]

We returned to the Shameen for breakfast, and then to the English service in the Episcopal Church.[38]

After luncheon I accompanied my host and hostess for a long pleasant walk on the city walls, obtaining most

---

37   Gordon-Cumming begins the day by attending the morning mass for Chinese women at the Sacred Heart (Shishi) French Cathedral in Guangzhou. There is a long description of the mass and the differences between the Catholic and Protestant churches as Gordon-Cumming sees them. She then returns to the home of her host and hostess (who she never names, unfortunately) on Shameen Island. For a full description of the Sacred Heart Cathedral see the China Revisited book 3, *Ling-Nam* by Benjamin Couch Henry.

38   The "Shameen" being the only hotel on Shameen Island, later better-known as the Victoria and today the Guangdong Victory Hotel. The 'Canton British Episcopal Church', or Christ Church, is now known as the Shamian Church on Shamian South Street. It was built around 1864, replacing an earlier church that had burned to the ground in 1856.

interesting views of the densely crowded city within and of the lines of intersecting wall which divide it into the various anti-fire wards. We wandered on for about three miles, passing the Flowery Pagoda, the Canton and Whampoa Pagodas, and finally reached a five-storied building to the summit of which we climbed, and so obtained another excellent view of the surroundings.

We also visited a temple with a green-tiled roof, in which an object of interest is a sacred black wooden dog with one horn on its forehead. It is adorned with votive offerings on pink cloth.

We were not sorry to avail ourselves of our strong human ponies for the return journey, especially as I had trysted to accompany Mrs Chalmers to an evening service at a private house in the city, where the missionaries of all denominations, who have all day been teaching in Chinese, meet every Sunday evening to worship together in English.[39] We walked along the canal and through the city, just at sunset, and found about forty persons assembled for a nicely conducted and hearty service.

---

39 Presumably they took sedan chairs. Mrs Chalmers being the wife of the Reverend John Chalmers (1825–1899), a Scotsman in Guangzhou with the London Missionary Society (LMS) and the first English translator of Lao Tzu's *Tao Te Ching*.

At its close we walked back through the very dark streets, with apparently no reason for any anxiety, the people being all quite civil. Some of the streets lighted with painted glass or horn lamps, silk-fringed, or gay paper lanterns, were most picturesque, and as full of busy shop-life as when we started in the morning. In some places we came on crowds gambling for cash or small pieces of food.

As we emerged from the closely packed houses to the street facing the canal, a great yellow moon was rising, and reflected on the waters, where lie many house-boats, each the home of a family.

We paused awhile to watch the scene, but a chilling miasma floated up from the waters, bidding us hurry onward, wondering how the boat-children escape croup and diphtheria!

Tuesday, 14th Jan.

I have had the good fortune to have a long day in the city with Dr Chalmers of the London Mission, who, having been at work here for a quarter of a century, and having a keen interest in the matters and customs of the land in which he lives (which is by no means a necessary sequence of long residence!), is a delightful companion on such a ramble, and I need scarcely say that really to enjoy such an expedition, one must go quietly on foot, with all powers of observation on the alert, never knowing what strange novelty will entail a halt at any moment.

We started at sunrise, but already the tide of busy life was well astir in the narrow streets of shops, through which we walked on our way to the great market for jade-stone, which is held daily at early morning in the open air near the temple of the Five Hundred Disciples, and closes before ordinary mortals are astir.[40]

Considering the extraordinary value which attaches to this precious mineral, I was chiefly amazed at the enormous quantity which we saw offered for sale. Not only is the market itself (a very large square building) entirely filled with stalls exclusively for the sale of objects manufactured from jade, but many of the surrounding streets are lined with open booths and shops for the same object; and truly, though every Chinese woman who can possibly obtain a jade ornament delights in it, as a European or an American glories in her diamonds, the prices are so prohibitive that it is difficult to imagine how a sale can be obtained for such a mass of bracelets and brooches, ear-rings and finger-rings, and especially of very ornamental pins for the hair.

---

40   Now invariably known as the Hualin Temple and founded in the sixth century AD.

Here poor women and middle-class tradesmen who cannot afford the genuine article solace themselves with imitation gems of green glass, or some such composition, which take the place of spurious diamonds, and effectually deceive the untrained eye. But at this market, I believe, only the genuine article is sold. We saw specimens of very varied colours, from a semi-opaque cream or milky-white tint to the clearest sea-green, or a dark hue the colour of bloodstone.

I am told that it is all imported from the Kuen-luen mountains in Turkestan, where there are mines of this mineral – the only mines in the worlds which are worked, so far as is known.[41] It has thence been brought to China as an article of tribute from the earliest times of which even the Celestials have any record, and so highly have they prized it that they have jealously striven to keep it entirely in their own hands. It is, however, thought possible that as this mineral is not known to occur anywhere in Europe, jade-celts, which have been found in European lake-swellings, and other pre-historic remains, have probably travelled thither as barter, in the course of the great Aryan westward migration from the highlands of Central Asia. Tradition affirms that the Aryans regarded the wearing of a jade ornament as the most effectual charm against

41   The Kunlun Mountain range spanning Tibet, Qinghai and Xinjiang.

lightning, a faith which would naturally account for their carrying with them many such treasures.

***

A large amount of the jade offered for sale in the market is quite in the rough, and here the lapidaries come to select such pieces as seem likely to be sound and of good colour throughout. It is extremely interesting to see these men at work in their primitive shops, which form a whole street by themselves. First the rough block is placed between two sawyers, who saw it in two by the horizontal movement of a saw of steel wire, with bow-shaped handle. From time to time they drop a thin paste of emery powder and water along the line they purpose cutting. These reduced portions are then passed on to other men, who work with small circular saws, and thus fashion all manner of ornaments.

Not very far from this street, there is one wholly inhabited by silk-weavers, whose hand-looms are of the most primitive description. A little further lies a curious street, a sort of Chinese Venice, where the houses edge a canal so closely that the people step from their doors into boats. This canal runs straight to one of the water-gates, by which all the market-boats enter the city every morning. These gates, being the portals beneath which the canal flows through the city walls, are closed at night, so all boats arriving after sunset must lie outside till morning; and great is the rush when at sunrise the portcullis is raised, and each boat seeks to enter first.

Among the produce thus brought to the daily market are sucking-pigs in search of a mother, as Chinese farmers do not care to allow one mother to suckle more than a dozen little piggies, whereas bountiful nature occasionally sends a litter nearly double that number. So whenever the births exceed the regulation limit, a litter of the supernumeraries is conveyed to the sucking-pig market, which is held daily in the early morning, and there the farmer whose sties have not been so abundantly blessed, buys a few of the outcasts to make up his number. But lest the maternal sow should object to adopting the little strangers, her own babies are taken from her, and placed with the new-comers, when all are sprinkled with wine. When the combined litter is restored to the anxious parent, she is so bamboozled by the delightful fragrance of the whole party, that she forgets to count them (or fears she may be seeing double), so she deems it prudent "to keep a quiet sough," as we say in the north, and accepts the increased family without comment![42]

Of course, in passing through the shop streets I could not resist many a halt, while my good guardian,

---

42 Gordon-Cumming means the "north" of England here obviously.

with inexhaustible patience, explained to me the use or meaning of sundry objects which to me were all strange curios. In many of the shops an unusual willingness to sell goods at reasonable prices indicates the approach of the New Year, as do also the number of street-stalls for the sale of small curios, inasmuch as it is a positive necessity for all accounts to be settled before the close of the Old Year, and therefore a tradesman will sometimes even sell at a loss, in order to realise the sum necessary to meet his liabilities. Should he fail to do so, he is accounted disgraced, his name is written on his own door as a defaulter, his business reputation is lost, and no one will henceforth give him credit.

***

We wandered from shop to shop, and from temple to temple, till I was fairly bewildered. But one scene remains vividly before my memory as the finest subject for a picture that I have seen in Canton. It is in the western suburbs, close to the temples of the Gods of War, and of Literature, and of the Queen of Heaven (in one of which I was especially fascinated by the multitude of small figures, carved and gilt, which adorn the roof, the sides of the temple, and the altar). Standing on the temple-steps, you look along the street, and combine a picturesque bridge with an arched gateway of the fire-wall spanning the highway. It is in such a quiet quarter, that I think I shall be able to secure a drawing of the scene.

***

Jan. 17th.

The masked fancy-ball came off last night, and was very amusing. There were nearly fifty people – some very pretty characters and some very funny ones. Most of the gentlemen wore Chinese masks for the first half-hour. The young ladies in the pagodas were highly successful, but ere long found their tall prisons so very hot that they were allowed to transgress all rules, and "come out" before their time.

Each day slips by full of many interests, even when we go no further than the limits of this green isle, but sit watching the infinitely varied boats or junks gliding past with their great brown or yellow sails; or else, at sunset, doing "joss-pigeon," throwing burning gilt paper into the river, as an offering to the Water Dragon, firing noisy crackers to keep off evil spirits, or lighting sweet incense-sticks and candles to place on the tiny boat altar.[43]

---

43 The "green isle" being Shamian. "Joss-pigeon" being the practice of lighting a bunch of joss sticks.

I often linger on the embankment to watch these, till I am conscious of a cold mist rising, and am glad to retreat to a cheery fireside – not without a thought of pity for the children who can never know the meaning of that word.

Jan. 18th.

***

All these thousands of boats which lie moored in compact phalanx along the shores of the river (at the mouths of creeks which are little better than sewers), get their water-supply by just dipping their bucket overboard, although they could easily obtain comparatively pure water in mid-stream! And this terribly unclean water is used unfiltered for all cooking purposes!

Considering our own terrible experiences of how luxurious homes in Britain have been left desolate by a draught of sparkling water into which, all unheeded, some taint of drainage had filtered, or even from the use of milk-vessels washed in such water, it does seem amazing that all this goes on with impunity, and that the whole population does not die wholesale in consequence a wonderful proof of the safeguard of only drinking boiled water, as is the Chinese invariable custom, in the form of tea.

We have plenty of opportunities for watching these people. As the boats lie moored around us in every direction, so that even without our leaving the shore they are always before our eyes, and whenever we go on an expedition on the river, we necessarily pass through crowds of boats, innumerable and indescribable, and some are very ornamental. Of their number some idea may be formed from the fact that the boating population of Canton alone is estimated at three hundred thousand persons, who possess no other home – whose strange life from their cradle to the grave is spent entirely on the rivers, with the dipping of the oars, or the tremulous quiver of the long steering-scull, as the ceaseless accompaniment of all life's interests. This is especially true of the women, who work the boats, for many of the men work on land all day, only returning at night to the tiny but exquisitely clean floating home which, though barely twenty feet in length, probably shelters three generations!

These are the sampans, or slipper-shaped boats with movable roofs of rain-proof bamboo basket-work.

Somewhat different from these are the boat-homes of sailors who are absent for months on long voyages on board the ocean-going junks, who return year after year, to find the home in which they were probably born, moored in the self-same spot in one of the multitudinous water-streets, for every boat has its own appointed anchorage; and the municipal regulations affecting the water-population are most minute, and strictly carried out, as indeed must be necessary where so enormous a community is concerned.

For this purpose a special river-magistrate has command of a strong body of water-police, who live in police-boats, and are bound to row about all night, blowing on shrill conch-shells, which are most effectual for awakening peaceful sleepers, and for giving notice of their approach to all evildoers, more especially to those very daring river-pirates from whose depredations they are bound to protect the public.

These water-constables, however, enjoy a very evil reputation, and are said frequently to be in league with malefactors, accepting bribes from pirates to keep well out of the way when any unusual deed of darkness is in prospect, such as capturing a wealthy citizen while crossing the river at night, and carrying him off as a prisoner until a large ransom can be extracted from his relations, which is one of the cheerful possibilities in these parts!

Still more frequently, however, the guardians of the peace are said to levy blackmail on their own account, helping themselves gratis from the market-boats, whose proprietors dare not complain, lest they should be falsely accused of some offence, which would lead to their prosecution and imprisonment, quite as certainly as if they were really guilty.

As regards cargo or passenger boats, fines, severe flogging, or imprisonment, or even a combination of all three, await the captain and crew of any boat which neglects to report its movements to the authorities, or which has the misfortune to lose any of its passengers. Should such a one fall overboard and be drowned, the boat or junk is compelled to lie-to or anchor till the corpse has been recovered. Grievous indeed, is the lot of all concerned should a junk or boat capsize in a squall, more especially if it can be proved that her mast and sails exceeded the regulation size. If, under such circumstances, only one or even two passengers are drowned, the captain alone suffers; but should three perish, the vessel is confiscated, and not only the captain but every man of the crew is condemned to wear the ponderous wooden collar (the cangue) for thirty days, and then to endure a judicial flogging!

Our barbaric notion that the captain must be absolute autocrat of his vessel is by no means allowed in China, where the law provides that in the event of an approaching storm, the passengers may require the captain to strike sail and wait till the danger is past. Should he refuse to comply with the requirements of the landlubbers, he is liable to receive forty blows of a bamboo! But terrible as are the Chinese floggings, they are mere trifles compared with the penalty of enduring the tortures of a Chinese prison, as a sequence to shipwreck!

I notice one class of boat which seems to ply a very busy trade, namely, that of the river-barbers, who devote themselves exclusively to shaving and head-scraping their floating customers. Each barber has a tiny boat in which he paddles himself about in and out among the crowd of sampans, attracting attention by ringing a little bell.

The river-doctor likewise gives warning of his whereabouts by means of a bell, so that as he goes on his way he can be called to any one needing his services.

There is not a phase of life on land which has not its counterpart on the river, and every variety of boat has its distinctive name. To begin with, there are whole fleets of market boats, each of which supplies the boating population with some one article. There are oil boats and firewood boats, rice boats and sugar-cane boats, confectioners' boats, shrimp boats, and fish boats; boats for sundry meats, and for pork in particular; boats for the sale of crockery, of salt, or of clothing. Some boats advertise their cargoes by a realistic sign hung from the mast-head – such as an earthenware jar, an oil-cask, a bundle of sugar-cane or of firewood, that their customers may espy them from afar.

There are floating kitchens, provided with an extensive brick-work cooking-range, where most elaborate dinners are cooked; these are served on board of floating dining-halls euphoniously called "flower boats," which are most luxuriously fitted up and highly ornamental, resplendent with a wealth of beautiful wood-carving, often brightly coloured and heavily gilt, and always brilliantly illuminated.[44] These are hired by wealthy citizens who wish to give their friends dinner-parties, as it is not customary to do so at their own homes except on great family festivals; such dinner-parties are enlivened by the presence of richly-attired singing-women. Poorer people find one end of the floating kitchen fitted up as a cheap restaurant or tea-house.

There are also some floating hotels, which are chiefly for the accommodation of persons arriving after the gates of the city are closed, or who merely wish to trans-ship from one vessel to another. Similar house-boats are hired by wealthy Chinamen as cool summer-quarters, or for going on expeditions. For pleasure excursions there are Hong boats answering to Venetian gondolas, with large comfortable saloons adorned with much carving and

---

44   Gordon-Cumming is obviously being slightly coy, or else was unaware, of the other, more intimate, services often being offered on the "flower boats"!

gilding, but so arranged as to be able to hoist a mast and sail.

In striking contrast with these gay boats, are the dull unattractive ones which we may term floating biers, as they are used only for conveying the dead to their place of rest. For though the dwellers on the land allow the boat people no homes ashore during their lifetime, they dare not refuse the dead a resting-place in the bosom of the earth.

Far sadder than these biers, for those whose weary life-struggle is ended, are the leper boats, tenanted by such of the boat-folk as are afflicted with leprosy, that most terrible of diseases, and who are therefore outcasts, forced to live apart from their fellows, and only allowed to solicit alms by stretching out a long bamboo pole, from the end of which is suspended a small bag (just as was done in medieval days by the lepers in Holland, as described in Evelyn's Diary AD 1641, when he noted "divers lepers poor creatures dwelling in solitary huts on the brink of the water," who asked alms of passengers on the canals by casting out a floating box to receive their gifts).[45] Of course these boats are deemed as wholly unclean as their inmates. Hence when in 1847 six young English merchants had been brutally murdered at a village in the

45 *The Diary of John Evelyn* (1620-1706), first published in 1818.

neighbourhood of Canton, the crowning insult to the hated foreigners was to return the mangled corpses to Canton in a common leper boat.

Then there are ecclesiastical boats, for though each dwelling-boat has its domestic altar, the public service of the gods is by no means omitted. So a large number of the Taouist priests have stationary boat-houses for themselves and their families, the chief saloon being dedicated to sundry Taouist idols.[46] These priests are liable at any moment to be summoned on board other boats to perform religious ceremonies on behalf of the sick, especially such as are supposed to be possessed of evil spirits. They also officiate in floating temples, in which elaborate services are performed on behalf of the souls of drowned persons, or of such beggar-spirits as have been neglected by their descendants.

During these "masses for the dead" the floating shrine is decorated with many white and blue banners, flags, and draperies, to indicate mourning. At other times the flags and decorations are of the gayest, and a band of musicians with shrill pipes and drums produce deafening sounds, all of which tell that the temple has been engaged by two families of the boat community for the solemnisation of a wedding; for in their marriage, as in all else, these people live wholly apart from those who dwell on land, and

---

46   "Taouist" being more commonly Taoist.

although the women are a much nicer, healthier-looking lot than those we see ashore, such a thing as intermarriage is unknown; the boat population being greatly despised.

But of all the multitudinous boats, perhaps the strangest are the duck and geese boats, some of which shelter as many as two thousand birds, which are purchased wholesale at the great duck and geese farms, and reared for the market. After seeing these boats, I no longer wondered at the multitude of these birds in the provision markets, where they form one of the staple foods of the people.

Beyond the expense of buying the half-grown birds, the owner of the boat incurs none in rearing them as he simply turns them out twice a day to forage for themselves along the mud-shores and the neighbouring fields, where they find abundance of dainty little land-crabs, frogs, and worms, snails, slugs, and maggots. They are allowed a couple of hours for feeding and are then called back, when they obey with an alacrity which is truly surprising, the pursuit of even the most tempting frog being abandoned in their hurry to waddle on board. Never was there so obedient a school, and it is scarcely possible to believe that this extraordinary punctuality is really attained by the fear of the sharp stroke of a bamboo, which is invariably administered to the last bird.

This afternoon we went to a most interesting expedition up the river, and then turned aside into one of the many creeks to the village of Fa-tee, and thence onward in search of the great duck-hatching establishment, where multitudinous eggs are artificially hatched. The first we came to was closed, but the boatman told us of another farther on, so we landed and walked along narrow ridges between large flooded fields in which lotus and water-chestnuts are grown for the sake of their edible roots. Both are nice when cooked, but the collecting of these, in this deep mud, must be truly detestable for the poor women engaged in it.

CHINESE NEW YEAR

New Year's Day, Jan. 22nd.

The great festival is now fairly ushered in, and certainly there has been noise enough to secure a very lucky year, if noise will do it!

***

The festival is kept up for about a fortnight, during which there is much play and little work. In fact, all who can afford it devote a whole month to feasting and recreation and theatrical exhibitions. Public and private businesses are alike set aside as far as possible, and relaxation from all cares is the one thing aimed at.

The Seal of Office belonging to every mandarin is formally sealed up on the 20th day of the twelfth month, and so remains for one month, a "few blank sheets having been stamped ready for use in case of any sudden emergency, and marked with four characters in red ink, to prove that they actually were stamped before the festive day, when the seal was laid by, a day which is always observed with much feasting and rejoicing. In short, it is the beginning of the holidays.

Every house and temple in the city has undergone a regular house-cleaning; floors have been scoured, walls washed, and it is considered an especially lucky omen to sweep the house with a broom made of bamboo shoots. In rich men's houses carpets are laid down; the beautiful blackwood furniture is covered with crimson embroidered cloth; gorgeous gold and artificial flower ornaments, banners, scrolls, charmed words and characters, are hung up in the reception-rooms, which are also decorated with fragrant plants.

Last night all people, of whatever social degree, presented offerings and gave thanks at their domestic and ancestral altars for care vouchsafed during the year; joss-sticks were burnt, lamps and candles were kept burning brightly, and offering laid before the shrines; gongs were beaten, and an incessant discharge of fire-crackers kept up. These consist of red tubes containing gunpowder, resembling miniature cartridges, and fastened together in rows, which, being thrown on the ground, go off with a sharp report; or if one is fired, all the others go off in rapid succession, making much noise but little show. Being let off at intervals before every door to frighten away bad spirits, they produce an almost incessant and deafening noise, and fill the air with smoke and smell of gunpowder. If only the evil spirits have ears they must surely suffer as much as we, the unsympathetic white "barbarians," and flee anywhere to get beyond its reach!

Yesterday all who could afford it had a great family banquet, prolonged for many hours (the multitude of small dishes and wearisome succession of courses forming the great feature at a Chinese feast). Just before midnight fresh offerings are laid before the ancestral tablets, bonfires are lighted, presents made to servants and children, and those who possess new clothes put them on. All endeavour, at least, to have clean clothes for this occasion.

To foreigners the interest of the New Year festival begins and ends on its eve, when the streets are thronged with people all buying and selling, every one hoping to profit by his neighbour's necessities to drive hard bargains even in the purchase of flowers for the domestic altar! The street known as Curio Street is lined from end to end with a double row of street stalls, where much trash, and occasionally some good things, are offered for sale.[47]

Having spent the greater part of the day in wandering about the city, to see as much as possible of the Celestial manners and customs, we returned at night to see the great fair. Of course there was a dense crowd, but by

---

47 The Curio Street Gordon-Cumming refers to is now Yuansheng Xijie Street.

distributing our party in couples, we got through it very well. I had the good fortune to be pioneered by a son of Dr Chalmers, whose perfect knowledge of the language proved of considerable advantage, as we wandered through the strange lantern-lighted streets, where the gorgeous signposts are made more attractive by decorations of scarlet cloth and gold flowers. We wandered about for a couple of hours, in and out of temples and gardens and strange little shops, buying all manner of old treasures, which we stored in a basket which we had been recommended to bring for this purpose, as of course on such a night the purchaser must himself carry away his goods.

We got home just before midnight, but even from the quiet of the Shameen we could hear the roar of the fire-crackers from the river and the city, and it continued for some hours. Indeed, there can be little time for rest, for long before dawn, worship must be offered to the Gods of Earth and Heaven, and sacrifices prepared, which are laid on a temporary altar in an outer room. These consist generally of five or ten small cups of tea, the same of wine, also of divers vegetables, a bowl of rice with ten pairs of chop-sticks, an almanack of the New Year tied with red string for luck, two or more ornamental red candles, and a pile of loose-skinned mandarin oranges, which, from their name (Kek, meaning also "auspicious"), are considered a lucky emblem, and, as such, are given to all visitors.

After a salvo of noisy crackers to frighten evil spirits, the head of the household adores Heaven and Earth in the name of the assembled family, giving thanks for past protection, and craving blessings for the coming year. This act of adoration is followed by another *feu de joie* and the burning of much joss-paper and mock paper money.[48]

Worship must next be rendered to the Domestic Gods. Another set of offerings must be prepared; small cups of tea and wine, tiny bowls of rice and vegetables, lighted candles and incense, burning of mock money. No animal food is offered on this day and many families abstain from eating it, from reverence to the Spirits of Heaven and Earth.

The Deceased Ancestors of the family are then worshipped, and a third set of offerings must be paid; richly-dressed mandarins and ladies are carried along in their closely-shit sedan-chairs, and friends on meeting stand still and bow repeatedly, while affectionately shaking their own clenched fists. Sometimes sugar-canes are fastened on to a lady's chair as a symbol of goodwill to the friend she visits. As the gift is purely ceremonial, the sugar-cane is rarely detached, so it does for all her friends, and combines economy with courtesy! The visits are most ceremonious, involving reverential homage to all elders and superiors, from juniors and inferiors.

---

48   *Feu de joie* being a form of formal celebratory gunfire.

Relatives of a family coming to call are led to the domestic altar, where they worship the ancestral tablets. Then sweetmeats and cakes are handed round, and tea, with either an olive or an almond in each cup, for luck. Copper cash are strung on red twine to give away on New Year's morning, a red silk thread is plaited in the children's hair, and small packets of cash or of melon seeds are tied up in red paper to give friends. Presents of eatables are sent to friends; buckets of the lucky loose-skinned orange, and cakes of cocoa-nut, small seeds, and sugar fried in oil, made up into brown balls. These were given to us at the house of a wealthy noble, whose very kindly wife and daughters, seeing that we thought them nice, not only insisted on filling our mouths with very large pieces, but sent a large basketful home with us. We see innumerable roast pigs and fowls being carried along the streets, either as gifts to the living or offerings to the dead, or to the gods.

About noon we went for a walk through the streets, usually so busy, but they seemed as if under a spell, all asleep. After the noise and hubbub of last night, this stillness was the more remarkable – it almost seemed as if my memories of the bewildering throngs in the midnight fair had all been a strange dream! Almost every shop was shut, for it is considered an unlucky omen to buy or sell on the New Year, and poor indeed must be the man who will do so. Certainly we did see some very respectable clothes shops open, and others selling sweetmeats and other food; still these are very exceptional, and most shops remain closed for several days. Indeed the longer they can afford to do so the more highly are they esteemed by their neighbours, for this is a sure proof of prosperity.

The deserted streets are all red with the remains of the paper fire-crackers let off last night; and as to certain temples we visited, their floors are literally strewn ankle-deep with the relics of the midnight battle fought with the devils! We went in and out of various fine buildings to see their decorations. One large establishment is a sort of dispensary for giving medical advice gratis to the poor – such funny medical advice! Its rooms are separated by very handsome open-work wood-carving. A little further we came to a merchant's guild, and found its grand hall so decorated as to resemble a temple – with images and a temporary altar covered with imitation fruit and little parcels of cash tied up in red paper as luck-pennies. The altar was decorated with huge bunches of gold flowers, and beside it stood a splendid state umbrella of crimson satin embroidered in gold. In short, everything suggested festivity; but as to the human beings, they were apparently all asleep after the fatigues of night and morning.

This afternoon we strolled as far as the Bund, but even the boating population seemed to be all sleeping, and no wonder!

Jan. 24th.

This is my last day in this most quaint, fascinating city. I have been for a farewell look at some of its most remarkable temples, and most characteristic streets. Especially we have visited the great sight of the day – namely, the New Year Toy Market for Children, gay with images floating on silver clouds, paper and gold flowers, and all manner of cheap playthings – a perfect paradise for the little ones, who mustered strong in their gayest clothes. The tiny ones look so funny with their odd little embryo plaits, sticking out like small horns on each side of the head.

There are also markets in the open street for the sale of paper lanterns of every conceivable form; flowers and fruits, butterflies and dragon-flies, birds, fishes, and animals, dragons, pigs, horses, crabs, monstrous human heads, &c. One very pretty form is that of five butterflies so arranged as to form a square lamp. In some, quaint processions of figures are made to move round and round by the action of heated air.

This feast of lanterns continues for a fortnight. Parents who have been blessed with offspring in the past year, buy lamps and present them as thanks-offerings at the neighbouring temples. Those who crave additions to their family also buy lanterns, to which they attach their names. They present them to one of the temples, where they are lighted from the sacred fire of the altar-lamps and suspended for some days, after which they are sent back to the house of the suppliant, to be suspended before his domestic shrine, above which are placed small waxen images of the gods of rank, happiness, and long life.

There are at this time all manner of processions in the streets at night, when men and women are dressed to represent characters in ancient Chinese stories; sometimes a monstrous dragon is represented, but he more resembles a centipede, the legs of the men who move him being plainly visible! These, with torch and lantern-bearers to swell the show, are among the amusements of the evening, which must really be exceedingly attractive, as the narrow streets are all illuminated with gay lamps suspended from beams which go right across from roof to roof, and are decorated with draperies of bright-coloured stuffs, hung in festoons.

On some of these festivals there are very remarkable fireworks, in which dragons are shown vomiting flames, rockets burst to descend in a shower of pagodas, amid wonderous coruscations of gold and silver fire – in short, the scenic effects are said to be as varied as they are effective.

But I might linger here for months without exhausting the interests of this strange city, and now I must devote a few days to the old Portuguese settlement of Macao.[49]

---

49   Gordon-Cumming adds her own footnote here at the end of her sections on Hong Kong and Guangzhou explaining why she has sadly omitted her impressions of Macao from *Wanderings in China:* 'Macao, with its old-world religious life, was to me most fascinating. Like some old English cathedral towns it is suggestive of a still back-water on life's rushing river. But space is limited – China is a vast subject, and Macao is so essentially un-Chinese, that I have decided to omit the letters referring to it.'

HONG KONG RACES

Wednesday, 19ᵗʰ Feb.

Hong-Kong certainly has good reason to appreciate its own race-course, for a prettier scene could not possibly be imagined.[50] This is the evening of the third day. Mrs Coxon being one of the very people here who cares for the exertion of driving a pony instead of being carried by men, drove me out cheerily early each morning in her little pony-carriage, which, I think, was the only wheeled vehicle in the vast assemblage.[51] Every one else went in

---

50   Gordon-Cumming is referring to the Happy Valley race-course, built in 1846.

51   Mrs Louisa Coxon was the second wife of George Stackpole "GS" Coxon (1824-1907), a partner in Coxon and Layton, Bill and Bullion Brokers of Hong Kong, a jockey club steward and notable cricketer. He had a brother who also had a company in Hong Kong trading shares. Coxon profited in Hong Kong and in 1892 bought "Macomer", a house on the Peak Road (named after his father-in-law's property in Sardinia). Louisa was a founder of the Ladies' Recreation Club in 1883.

chairs, borne by two, three, or four men, as the case might be (Chinese law does not allow a Chinaman to have more than two bearers, unless he holds certain official rank, but foreigners generally think it necessary to have their chair with full complement of bearers, if they have occasion to go a hundred yards!)

Each morning the whole two miles to the race-course was one densely-packed crowd of human beings, one half of the road being absorbed by a double row of chairs and Chinese bearers, and the other half crowded with Chinamen, soldiers, sailors, native police, &c., all pouring along, intent on this grand ploy – such a quaint looking throng, yet all so perfectly orderly, they might be going to church or coming from it; and yet these Chinamen, with their impassive faces, are the most inveterate gamblers, and many a heavy stake has been lost and won in these three days. That two-mile long procession of chairs in double file was a sight in itself. The road is in itself a very pretty one; even the streets being partly overshadowed by large trees, and then the way lies along the bright blue sea. Indeed, blue is the predominant colour everywhere, for by far the greater part of the crowd are dressed in blue, indigo-dye being so cheap, and large blue cotton umbrellas find great favour.

The race-course itself is admirably situated, being a dead level embosomed in wooden hills, with a broad stream flowing to the blue sea, and the distant hills of the mainland seen through a gap. On either side of the Grand Stand are built a series of large, comfortable, thatched stands, which are the permanent property of the governor, the stewards of the races, and the different great mercantile houses, combining a luxurious dining-room on the ground-floor with a comfortable open drawing-room upstairs, furnished with any number of arm-chairs. The finest stand of all, with flat-terraced roof, is the property of the Parsees. The programme is, that each morning, "society" meets in the Grand Stand, and there remains till the pause allowed for luncheon, when all disperse to the various great luncheon parties in the private stands, and then spend the afternoon in the drawing-rooms aforesaid, where there is abundant supply of coffee and ices.

I followed out this pleasant programme for two days, and was vastly amused, but this morning I devoted to sketching the scene, so I resolutely forsook the many kind friends, and went off by myself to a hill in the "Happy Valley", the peaceful cemetery for all nations and sects, whence I could overlook the whole scene; and truly it was a pretty sight, with the amazing crowd of Europeans and Chinamen seeming no bigger than ants – blue ants – and such a swarm of them!

From this high post I saw the races to perfection, and especially enjoyed the excellent music of the 74th band and of their seven pipers, headed by Mackinnon, a Speyside man.[52] The music gained vastly as it floated up to me, every note clear, instead of the ear being distracted by all the jarring sounds of the race-course. (Apart from these, what a strange and aggravating phase of "entertainment" it is that so continually provides excellent music, and yet deems it necessary to add thereto the strain of conversation!) So this morning I had full enjoyment of "The Pibroch o' Donald Dhu," "Tullochgorum," and every so many more beloved old melodies, which were echoed by the hills around, and floated away through fir woods which might have clothed a Scottish hillside. I never heard any sound better than a bugle piece by Mackinnon's son, its notes just mellowed by distance.

But, truly, looking down from this point, it is a strange combination to see the semicircle of cemeteries and mortuary chapels, just enfolding the race-course and, as it were, repeating the semicircle formed by the Grand Stands!

---

52   i.e. the band of the 74th Highland Regiment which was stationed in Hong Kong in 1878 and part of 1879 before returning to its former posting of the Straits Settlements. William Mackinnon (1840-1918) was actually a Lanarkshire man, but of West Highland stock. He joined the 74th Highlanders in 1863 as a piper, soon becoming the regiment's Pipe Major.

Two days ago I chanced to wander into this silent God's Acre, just in time to witness a most lonely funeral. It was that of a European who had died unknown at the hospital. Four Chinese coolies carried his coffin, and the only other persons present were the parson and the sexton, neither of whom had known the poor fellow in life. It was the funeral of "somebody's darling," but not one mourner was near.

Tomorrow night there is to be the usual race ball, but ere then I expect to be far away at sea, as I embark for Foo-chow early in the morning.[53]

On Board the SS "Namoa,"[54]
Feb. 20ᵗʰ.

At 2pm this morning we were aroused by the wild clanging of the fire-alarm – a sound which I have happily not heard since the first night of my arrival, when it impressed itself so awfully on our senses.[55] Strange that my first and last

---

53   "Foo-chow" being Fuzhou.

54   The SS *Namoa* was a coasting steamer operated by the Douglas Steamer Company, which had only been formed in Hong Kong in 1883. The *Namoa's* routine run was between Hong Kong and Swatow (now Shantou).

55   This appears to be a typo and Gordon-Cumming means 2am.

night in Hong-Kong should be marked by such haunting memories! The house stands so high that it commands a wide view of the town, and looking out, we saw the flames rising from a point near the naval yard. Fortunately it did not turn out to be very serious, but Mr Coxon had to start instantly to join the fire-brigade (of which I think he is the captain). Curiously enough he was introduced to me, sitting on his fire-engine, the morning of that awful Christmas night, and this morning he came straight from his engine to the steamer to say good-bye!

Various other friends also came to speed their parting guest, for in the East the world is early astir, and wondrously warm-hearted. So my last memories of Hong-Kong were as pleasant as all the rest, and it was with true regret that I looked my last on that beautiful scene, bathed in the soft morning light.

APPENDIX

Wanderings in China: The Illustrations

The first volume of Gordon-Cumming's *Wanderings in China*, from which the above excerpts are all taken, contains few accompanying images and no maps. Volume 1 of *Wanderings in China* contains four images. They are *Hong Kong – City of Victoria; Junks and Sampans on the Min River; City of Foo-chow: Looking Toward the Arsenal and Mount Kushan* and *A Hill of Graves, Foo-Chow*.[56] The latter three pictures relate to descriptions of Gordon-Cumming's later travels in *Wanderings in China: Volume 1*. However, of the four illustrations only *Junks and Sampans on the Min River* contains Gordon-Cumming's signature, while the others remain anonymous.

The images are rendered in "autotype" in the book, a method pioneered by the Autotype Fine Art Company Limited of London who produced photomechanical

---

56   Foo-chow being Fuzhou and Mount Kushan being also known as Drum Mountain and the site of a celebrated Buddhist monastery.

prints (using the carbon process) and later photogravure. At the time autotype was considered a new technology greatly improving image reproduction in the book printing process.

As noted in the introduction Constance Gordon-Cumming was an accomplished painter, having begun as a child in Scotland. Reputedly her motto was 'never a day without at least one careful-coloured sketch' and an estimated one thousand watercolours have been attributed to her. During her lifetime her art was certainly more appreciated than her writing, which was often described as a random series of anecdotes without much point. Perhaps a not wholly incorrect criticism, though now at a century and a half's remove, Gordon-Cumming's anecdotes of Hong Kong and southern China provide a useful addition to the region's historical record.

Later in her career Gordon-Cumming's paintings would feature in a great number of exhibitions in both Britain and the United States. Examples of her watercolours are retained in the collections of a number of museums including the Honolulu Museum of Art, the Oakland Museum of California and the Yosemite Museum, as well as various collections and archives as far flung as Sydney and Edinburgh. Her work occasionally comes up for sale from private collections. Gordon-Cumming's London *Times* obituary in 1924 noted, 'She had very fair artistic taste and produced, as the result of her wide wanderings, many sketches, both in black-and-white and in colour, which she was always ready to exhibit whenever desired to do so.'[57]

The author's portrait – also reprinted in *Wanderings in China* – is from a photograph by William Cooke of 103 Princes Street, Edinburgh. Cooke was the most prominent professional studio photographer in Scotland at the time.

57 'Obituary – Miss Gordon-Cumming', *The Times* (London), September 5, 1924.

Also available in the *China Revisited* series:

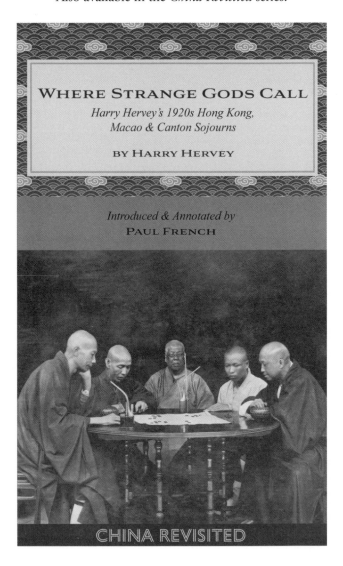

WHERE STRANGE GODS CALL

*Harry Hervey's 1920s Hong Kong,
Macao & Canton Sojourns*

BY HARRY HERVEY

Introduced & Annotated by
PAUL FRENCH

CHINA REVISITED

LING-NAM

*Hong Kong, Canton &
Hainan Island in the 1880s*

BY BENJAMIN COUCH "BC" HENRY

Introduced & Annotated by
PAUL FRENCH

CHINA REVISITED